BOI

Nicola Bray lives in London where she graduated from Royal Holloway's Creative Writing MA. Her poems were highly commended in the 2015 Faber New Poets scheme and in 2017 she was selected for the inaugural *Poetry London* mentoring scheme. *Boi* is her debut pamphlet.

Boi

Published by Bad Betty Press in 2021
www.badbettypress.com

Nicola Bray has asserted her right to be identified as the author of
this work in accordance with Section 77 of the Copyright, Designs
and Patents Act of 1988.

Cover design by Amy Acre

Printed and bound in the United Kingdom

A CIP record of this book is available from the British Library.

ISBN: 978-1-913268-18-3

Supported using public funding by
ARTS COUNCIL ENGLAND

Boi

BAD
BETTY
PRESS

Boi

Gender is the poetry each of us makes
out of the language we are taught.

—Leslie Feinberg

*For Michael, James, Anthony,
Jonny & Bliff*

Contents

Landscape

After Lili Elbe

In the history of medical arts I do not exist.
The archive is destroyed.

A simple white frame illuminates my skin.

Hands clasped, neck and jaw one continual line,
painted bow mouth and my eye drawn

to the muscles in my face, the cut of this shirt,
the false unevenness of these breasts.

This landscape is a brute.

It is not with my brain, not with my eyes,
not my hands that I want to create

but with my heart and with my blood.
Lay your body over mine like a stencil,

know that nothing stranger will ever happen,
that nothing stranger could.

Paper Trail

ink memory i

The awkwardness, and call it that if you will,
of carrying a standard, the weight
causing a stoop of the shoulders
and a whole congregation – did I say this is a church –
font-washed in mother's milk,
a tidy white and red carnation, Baby on a shelf.

Mother is short,
dusty and practical, walking the length
and breadth of her sideboard
cock-a-hoop and flaunty,
rouging her cheeks with a good deal of sugar,
the brisk wind of morning
and Baby swinging from the washing line.

ii

This is where you find me,
shaped like a crib,
a cry folded into doll's clothes.
Even in this unfamiliar house
you know the swell of me.

iii

December and it's dark outside.
I'm sitting on the top deck of the number 28
and in the same way that I can't hear
the city or see past the glass
it feels like a nose in unfamiliar hair,
the scent of something strange in a shop –
Pizza Pizza brilliantly lit
or breathing behind plastic.

iv

Clocks keep on ticking:
a square-nosed dog, a dog
with a tubular neck,
a clockwork dog, small ears,
wiry coat, short legs,
and when it walks, dog-like,
into the toy room, and it does,
the skies fill with albatross,
school term comes to an end.

v

The girl in the opposite hospital bed
has a bag on her head;
tonight I stay up late
shrieking like a hinge or lung,
grinding my chin on streaks of silver –
the doctors say *inhale* and I do.
Of course that thing with the girl
and the bag looks medieval.

vi

There are cells in the histamine journal,
notes in the margin like crow militia
and plastic in the alleyways –
the rain knowing all along
this lah-di-dah circuit and shortness of breath
is just another pretty face,
oxygen and bubbles.

vii

The wet and slime of late afternoon
is fathoming paving slabs,
it's an oil-and-water girlish idea
to take a boy home.
Compare this to a smothered summer,
to grieving birdsong.

viii

I lie on the edge
of wakefulness,
clothes hanging like beautiful shadows
on the other side
of the room.

A first cigarette
on the lips of a kid
flat-chested and singular,
a dragonfly girl,
pale and oval.

When I inhale,
my body has a slightness
you may never
see again.

ix

The boi in me, short nails, *click-clack*
doodles with a pencil,
these days are shit in a prawn tail,
too flimsy to stick behind an ear.

What I want is Bakelite,
the certainty of lettering
because this quiz is familiar
like an engine turning over,
a disappearance or sudden death,
my books packed by another girl –
something like that.

This is a time of short stories.
I take against one in particular,
spend late afternoon stoning apricots,
soon I will be gone.

x

The road trip starts cross-legged,
short black hair, hot pants
from when I was a girl –
as if I remember.

xi

Leaning from the window, naked,
wrapping myself in curtain,
shaping smoke rings into the street,

I'm grey as mirror. Junkie crows wait,
the sun divides the horizon,
moody as my selfish DNA.

I've done this before, chased silver foil
as if it were a jewel – when a necklace is worn
too often eventually the twine splits.

Daughter, daughter, leave the sudden mist –
wish yourself mottled with the fabricated pattern
of a first summer dress.

Stones fall one by one
close to the bruises at my ankles;
this is where reflexology locates the fallopian tubes,

ovaries, womb, internal landscapes
where histories passing mouth
to mouth is shared breathing.

xii

Back in Earl's Court, wearing someone else's jeans
I call it moth light or moth wishes;

by now I'm restless, listening for the click of heels,
reflecting on my watery-self.

This time I'm laughing in shivers
and curves, forcing the river

to mirror my lips, the river is mine
and I'm not thinking of anything.

I'm sure I exist like a bird in a bible
trying to fly in a hundred different languages.

There's something about a day
underwater and being green and moody;

how the riverbank sounds like a break
in the week and you're forced to admire

my Saturday clothes. All of this,
and the stench of wine, shots, feathers.

xiii

Acrobats or capoeira?
Much could be made of this:
the sun on the Southbank, the shoes
I'm wearing and whether or not
I have the balls to kick them off.
I stand like a silhouette clearing its throat –
a dramatic illusion   stones I might slip on

                                        three spirit

                              rural queer
gender blind

                    boi

                        gay masculine off centre
other queer unicorn   pansexual

                  fluid tomboy

                              queer power bottom
provocateur lesbian daddy

dynamic playful   transqueer

queer butch trans top   in-betweener

gender queer butch baba wife

gold star butch daddy

daddy femme dyke dom queen   gay queer feminist

cisgender queer feminist butch queen

lesbian androgynous tomboy

cisgendered man

xiv

Slam the table three times
with the foot of a glass

Grappa should be sipped

straight to the heart!
Conversation folds like a napkin.
Folds into a linen swan or sailor's cap.

My finger and thumb dawdle too long
on the stem of the glass.

Take this credit card

Each number bears a symbol – one mother,
one daughter, the year I was born –

and at the next table a poet eating lunch,
who doesn't know my face
or the voice stencilled on white cloth.

Wear floral skirts, grow your hair long again

I'm sitting at the table splitting hairs,
splitting follicles for fun.
I can split one hair in two, I can do that.

xv

I leave the house,
leave the mirror. I'm on my way –

envisage the life of a firstborn son –
leave by a second door

to the cobble of late afternoon,
leave a radio playing

and crepe paper flowers –
it was like this then –

say, *wait here everyone,*
I'll be back in a minute or so.

I leave branches and holiday smiles,
pools of tepid water, half-a-chance

and the glory of rust, leave a palette of flesh
the colour of the tenements,

limbs in a wilderness
of mattresses and paper cups.

xvi

The reason for typing my name into Search?
That sometimes an afternoon is longer
than adolescent legs in old photographs,

trousers ha! Pure '79, a white denim statue,
cocky hands on hips, hair dark
and wonderful; a punky blue boi

laughing in waves of *yes go topless* –
four short syllables bitten from a coastline
with a raw-rock mouth. Now dressed as an acrobat

I balance on a timeline.
Really I'm a watch on a young man's wrist,
an outline on skin that hasn't seen the sun.

xvii

I call it my centre of gravity.
It's not the cock in this canvas bag
or estrogen and testosterone,
more how I'm bound to the earth –
as if I'm a balancing ball in water.

xviii

The therapist turns her back to the screen,
a bedroom door knob continues to turn
and somewhere in London my green dress,
re-runs of my favourite film.

xix

This is the stuff of the universe,
easy as swimming in a womb.

I'm tethered to a long white ribbon.

Steps I painted blue last summer,
garden of white white white.

My name unravels. I hook it
from the water with a pitchfork.

My name slides slow-motion,
half-writhing, unwinding. Admire its ingenuity.

xx

The pharmacy's a pastoral scene
of walnut walls and bevelled glass –
looking back, it was Farrow & Ball,
half-world green and cow's milk cream –
trans folk come in herds.

xxi

It was a cruel winter.
Girls shone their faces in anyone's mirror
and their lipstick and lines were frozen fountains.
It was a cruel winter
and the pretty face of filigree was frosty.

It's nothing like the Titchmarsh TV show
or pressing my nose against filthy glass:
I watch all of this
through the lenses in the glasses
of the guy beside me on the train.

There's a woman speaking loudly on her mobile.
Obscured by someone's shoulder,
she's a disembodied voice.

xxii

Leicester Square on Christmas Day
and if there's a thought the colour of steel benches
it's something of inherited body.

There's nothing here that isn't grey as pigeon –
the monochrome moon has the sadness
of subways. There's always a tremor
in chords and trains.

xxiii

This morning a bird –
black wings, white feathers, fringes of yellow –
flew into this house, a house of glass
and that is straightforward enough;
a bird looking for a gap,
tapping its beak in the echoing echo,
making sense of sound like telephone pips,
put a coin in the slot, reverse the charge
to when you could reverse the charges.

Yes, this is straightforward, look at my face in the glass.
Hold a mirror up to the lake,
go back to putting curlers in,
back to counting stationery, drawing pins,
postcards with my name printed in the corner;
an old address, a new address.
Friends are leaving now,
their irises turning blue-green,
how dull it is when eyes turn inwards
and the milky rain is suddenly paler and paler.

This goddess of uneven thought
is cast from cheap metal, a fake candelabra
with an awkward arm because
this is when I am a girl chewing hat elastic –
Year 9, Year 10,
the year mother forgot how to sew
and I learnt how to stitch,
moved from ballet shoes to caps,
O the satin and the sex.

And one afternoon music in next door's bedsit,
feet on the stairs to a landing of lovers,
a mobile hanging over the bath,
flickering water, a telephone ringing.
My belly is a land of wonder
shifted and kicked into shape.

xxiv

There are ginger toms on the fire escape
and curtains tied in knots.
Nine flights up my cigarette ash
is burning white
and the girl in the corner,
one I forgot, doesn't have a clue.
This could be New York,
a sketch pad in the Hotel Chelsea;
downstairs a woman is tipping
her mattress from the window;
jumping bugs live month by month
but all of this is bullshit
because most likely you are dead
and your neighbour is dead,
the flowers are dead and the playground
has stopped playing and the children
in the playground are married
and unhappy or married and kidding
themselves or having an affair;
in the flat downstairs
newlyweds are watching a TV show,
across the hall it's Monday,
a baby is born,
bird-boned and naked.

The sky is the colour of Pheno,
as if remnants of last night's circus
turn the world top-down and bottom-up.
The sun appears like a silver jug from behind
the trees, a new day or aspect is stirring.
Clouds are wearing surgical masks,
and I'm a first fingerprint,
a version at least but magnified,
a body worn by my alter, but this is incidental.
Ivy grows along the wall as flat as a stencil.
There are sprinkles from a hosepipe on a cobweb –
a morning of water and sunlight.

xxvi

I'm in the bath when my umbilicus appears.
Until this time, I imagine myself a loner
but immersed in water
my body resembles a land mass,
an inherited continent,
somewhere I've never been perhaps –
a place discovered in the creases of my skin
folding and darkening.

In the room across the hall
I hear the tapping of fingers
and then nothing. Someone leaves a bed,
switches on a television, turns a lever in the shower.
I think I hear water on skin, louder than the seas,
leaving a footprint, as if it had one.

xxvii

I'm sitting here watching shots on YouTube:
Hijra Wearing Yellow Lengha, the caption says,

Nhan, behind a Veil, framed by a mosquito net;
living with HIV in Cambodia;

A day at the beach June 1969, photographed with telescopic lenses;
Atascadero State Hospital. Then comes the O! of pain

a decade of lobotomies, a whitened sky.

What is it I say at the top of a hill when the sky fills with geese:
my voice in my mouth – simple as that.

I try to remember my marathon summer,
the further I ran the older I became until I was quite the man.

I kept my teeth, lost my hair, it turned up as a fur ball
at the back of my throat. I made a mammal's coat,

woke in perfectly fitted skins.

xxviii

For now a metal bedframe,
some condensation or breath,
for now, the buckle and belt of a tightening strap
and bumping bumping
a suitcase down the stairs.

On the other side of the window
a child at a table –
his square shoulders and beautiful bones
like naked branches

and even if this were something new,
different trees, trees facing the door –
a door that is always ajar.
He speaks a composition of crazy violins.

He's learning to walk in Capital Letters,
learning to spell a name
he's not sure is his.

Version

I'm fishlike: more than this stroke on stroke,
passing through bubbles of sound, I'm my own

version of evolution. With boyish determination
I plunge deeper but whose idea was it to swim?

The tautology of blue swimming shorts reduces me
to childhood. I breathe in waves, call out

to ripples of small pelagic fishes and still these feet
can't reach the sea bed, my shoulders bobbing. Above

a frenzied concentricity of gulls, a looping umbilicus
in a silver void. Timeless where all name is folly.

Birds calling like spirits, calling like ancestors,
gasping for air, heads thrown back.

Acknowledgements

This pamphlet is dedicated to the memory of Eileen and Mervyn O'Gorman.

Grateful thanks to the editors of *Magma* and *The Rialto* in which these poems were first published, sometimes in different forms.

'Landscape' appeared as part of *Magma*'s online feature on its pamphlet competition.

Sections *xiv, xvi, xxiii, xxv* and *xxvii* of 'Paper Trail' appeared in *The Rialto*.

A very big thank you to Jake and Amy for giving *Boi* a home. Amy enabled me to see my work with new eyes, she's a brilliant editor and I've loved working with her.

Thank you to Ahren Warner, Colette Bryce and the team at *Poetry London* for an invaluable year.

Thank you to Richard Scott for his generous teaching and encouragement and for his kind words.

A special thank you to Bill Greenwell and my friends at the Poetry Clinic. Bill has been a constant source of support and encouragement for many years and for this I'm hugely grateful.

Lastly to mum for her inspiring stories, to dad, to my brother Michael and partner Donna.

Lightning Source UK Ltd.
Milton Keynes UK
UKHW010641020821
388172UK00002B/400

9 781913 268183